HOLIDAY SCROLL SAWING
PATTERN COLLECTION

©2017 by Fox Chapel Publishing Company, Inc., 903 Square Street, Mount Joy, PA 17552.

Holiday Scroll Sawing Pattern Collection is an original work, first published in 2017 by Fox Chapel Publishing Company, Inc. The patterns contained herein are copyrighted by the authors. Readers may make copies of these patterns for personal use. The patterns themselves, however, are not to be duplicated for resale or distribution under any circumstances. Any such copying is a violation of copyright law.

ISBN 978-1-56523-932-6

Printed in USA
First printing

COMPOUND-CUT
Icicle Snowmen

By Sue Mey
Cut by Leldon Maxcy
Painted by Kristen Scanlan

Materials & Tools

Materials:
- Wood, 1¾" (4.4cm) square: assorted lengths from 4" to 6¾" (10.2cm to 17.1cm)
- Masking tape
- Adhesive: spray or glue stick
- Packaging tape
- Sandpaper
- Paint: white acrylic or spray
- Acrylic paints, paint pens, or permanent markers
- Fabric or yarn
- Screw eye

The author used these products for the project. Substitute your choice of brands, tools, and materials as desired.

Tools:
- Scroll saw blades: #9 skip-tooth
- Paintbrushes
- Drill with bits: assorted small

Sue Mey lives in Pretoria, South Africa. To see more of her work, including a wide variety of patterns and pattern-making tutorials available for purchase, visit www.scrollsawartist.com.

Icicle snowmen pattern

Enlarge to 133% or desired size.
Cut to assorted lengths as shown.

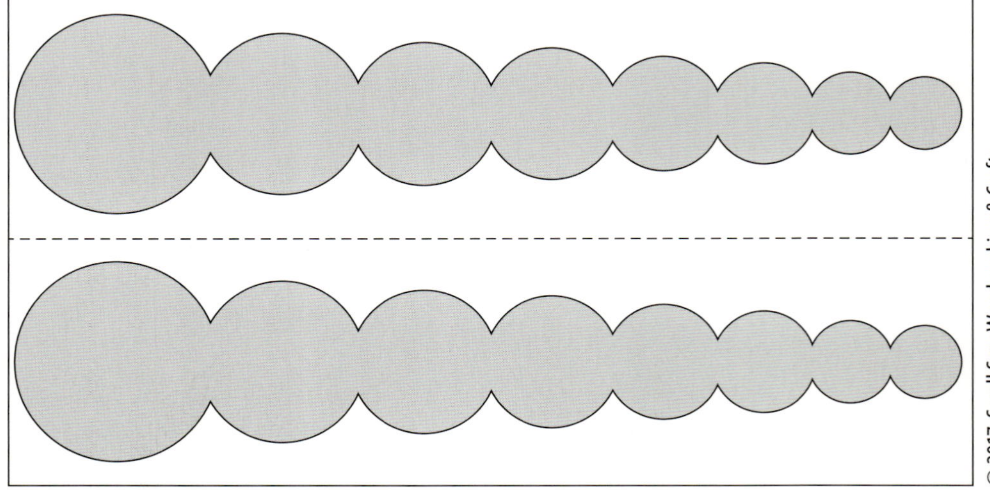

Snowflake
ORNAMENTS

By Jacob and Wayne Fowler

Snowflake ornament patterns

Enlarge to 125%
or desired size.

Jacob Fowler designed his first scroll saw project when he was five years old. He now spends most of his time designing fantasy and animal patterns. Wayne Fowler has published nearly 150 articles since 1998. His work has won awards at a local craft guild and several science fiction conventions.

Materials & Tools

Materials:
- White or light wood: ¼" (6mm) thick: 3" (7.6cm) square
- Sandpaper: 220 or 320 grit
- Spray adhesive: temporary-bond
- Tape: clear packaging
- Finish: oil
- Fishing line
- Drill press with bits: assorted small
- Sander (optional): belt or disc sander

Tools:
- Scroll saw blades: #3 reverse-tooth

The author used these products for the project. Substitute your choice of brands, tools, and materials as desired.

Santa Treat Plate Holder

By Paul Meisel

Materials & Tools

Materials:
- Wood, ¾" (1.9cm) thick: 6" x 35" (15.2cm x 88.9cm)
- Plywood, ¼" (6mm) thick: 3" x 7" (7.6cm x 17.8cm)
- Dowel, ³⁄₁₆" (5mm) dia.: 1" (2.5cm) long
- Dowel, ¼" (6mm) dia.: 1" (2.5cm) long
- Wooden ball knob, ¼" (6mm) dia. (#1801)*
- Wood screw: #8 x 1⅝" (4.1cm) long (#1410)*
- Sanding sealer
- Polyurethane finish
- Wood glue
- Paint marker: black (#1410)*
- Acrylic paint, such as Delta Ceramcoat*: black (#02506), white (#02505), red (#02507), green (#02421), flesh (#02126)

Tools:
- Scroll saw blades: #5 reverse-tooth
- Clamps
- Screwdriver
- Paintbrushes

The author used these products for the project. Substitute your choice of brands, tools, and materials as desired.

SPECIAL SOURCES:
The items above marked with an asterisk (*) are available from Meisel Hardware Specialties. Call 1-800-441-9870 or visit their website, www.meiselwoodhobby.com.

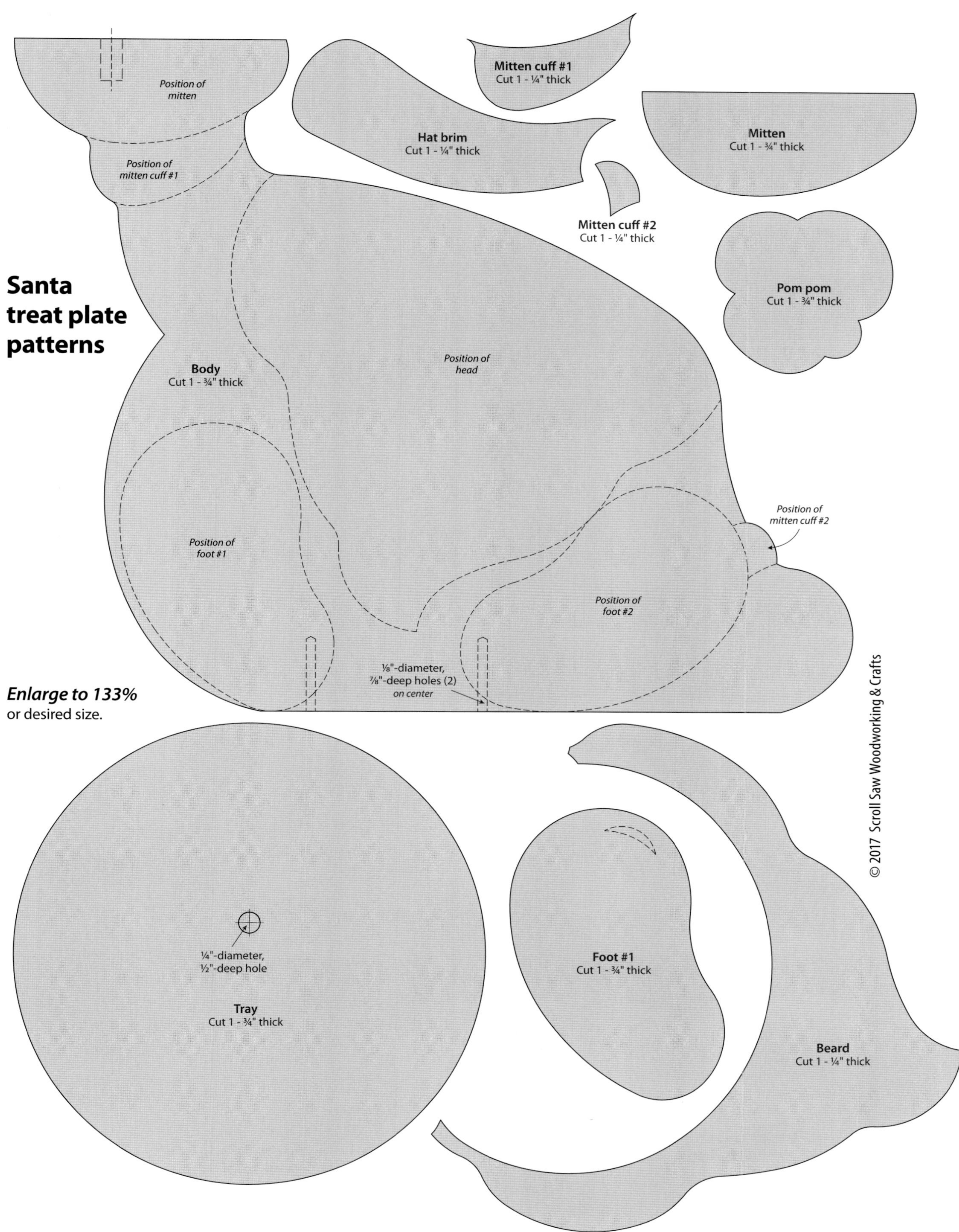

Position of mitten
Position of mitten cuff #1
Mitten cuff #1
Cut 1 - ¼" thick
Hat brim
Cut 1 - ¼" thick
Mitten cuff #2
Cut 1 - ¼" thick
Mitten
Cut 1 - ¾" thick
Pom pom
Cut 1 - ¾" thick
Santa treat plate patterns
Body
Cut 1 - ¾" thick
Position of head
Position of mitten cuff #2
Position of foot #1
Position of foot #2
⅛"-diameter, ⅞"-deep holes (2) on center
Enlarge to 133% or desired size.
¼"-diameter, ½"-deep hole
Tray
Cut 1 - ¾" thick
Foot #1
Cut 1 - ¾" thick
Beard
Cut 1 - ¼" thick
© 2017 Scroll Saw Woodworking & Crafts

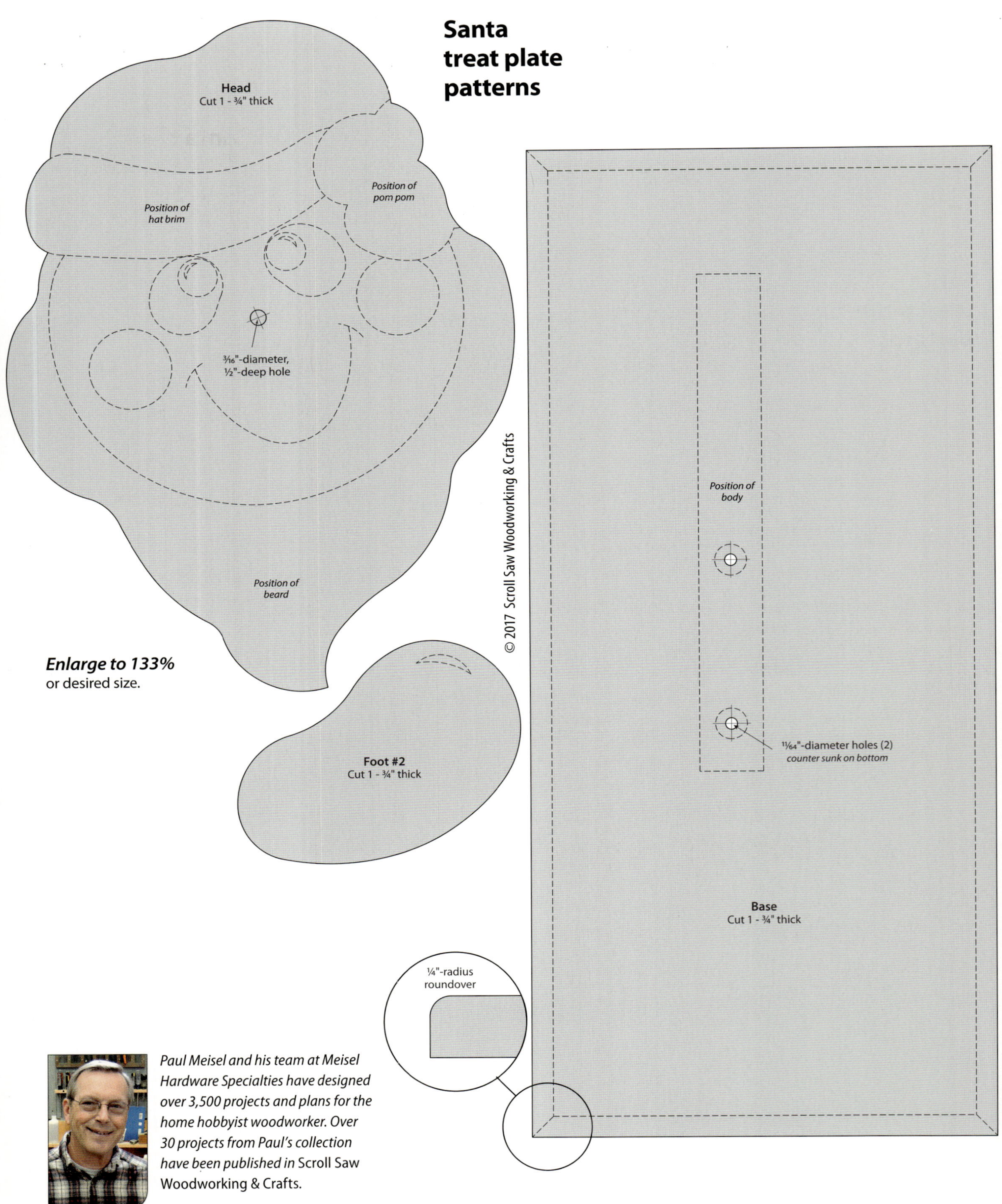

Paul Meisel and his team at Meisel Hardware Specialties have designed over 3,500 projects and plans for the home hobbyist woodworker. Over 30 projects from Paul's collection have been published in Scroll Saw Woodworking & Crafts.

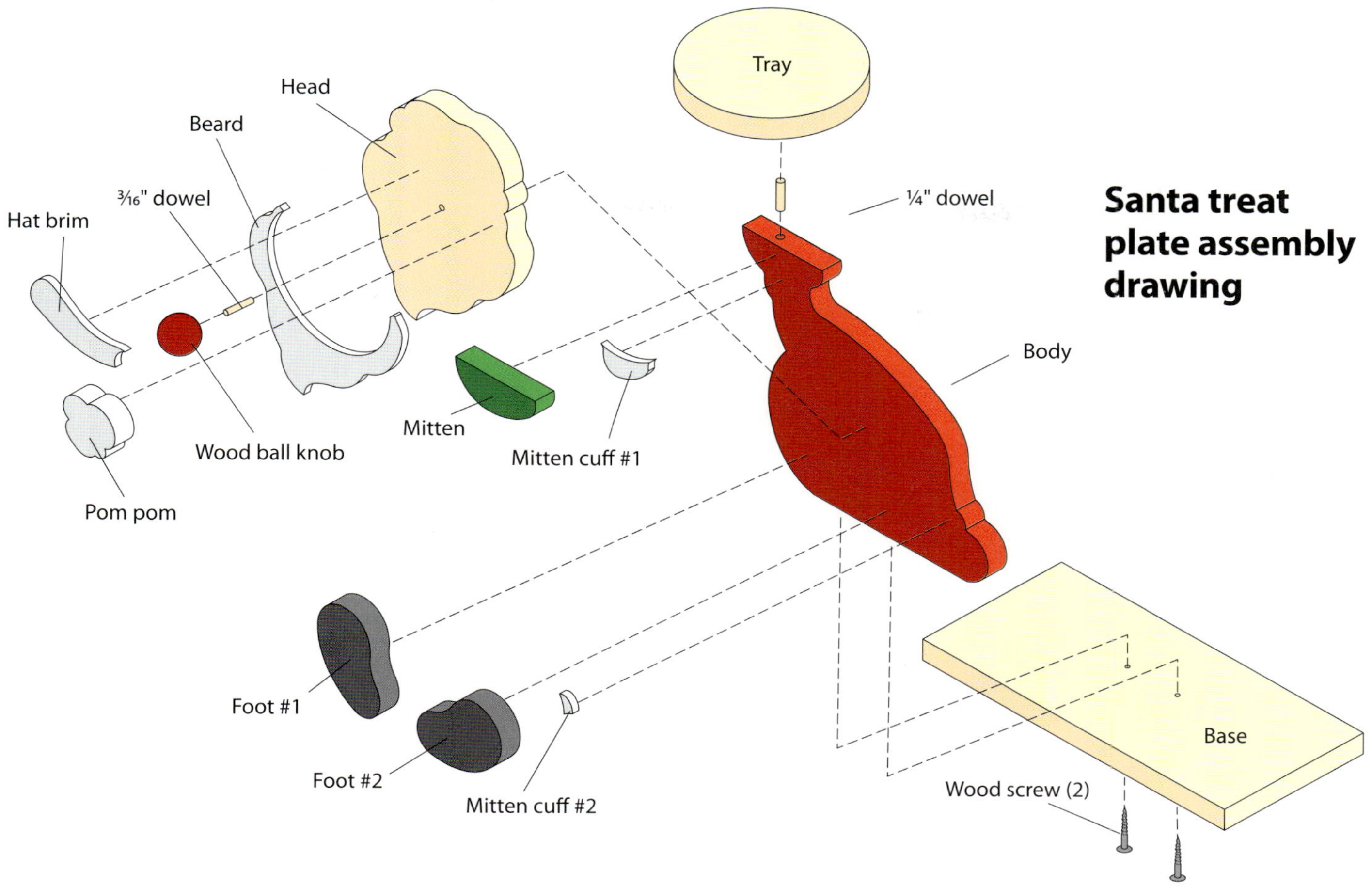

Santa treat plate assembly drawing

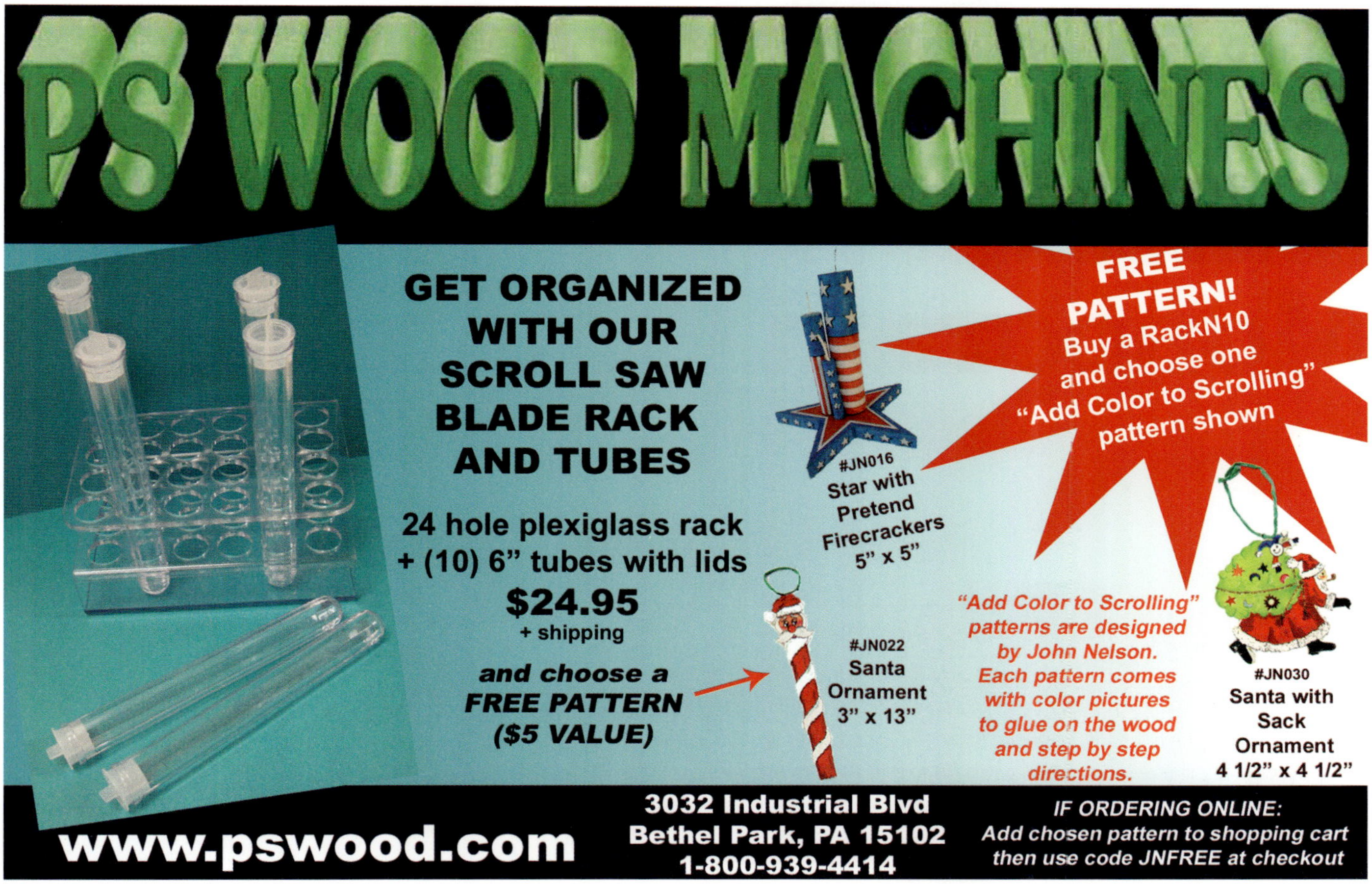

COMPOUND-CUT
Monogram Ornaments

By Sue Mey
Cut by Leldon Maxcy

Materials & Tools

Materials:
- Wood, 1¾" (4.4cm) square: 5¼" (13.3cm) long per ornament
- Masking tape
- Adhesive: spray or glue stick
- Packaging tape
- Sandpaper
- Finish, such as Danish oil

Tools:
- Scroll saw blades: #9 skip-tooth
- Paintbrushes
- Drill with bits: assorted small

The author used these products for the project. Substitute your choice of brands, tools, and materials as desired.

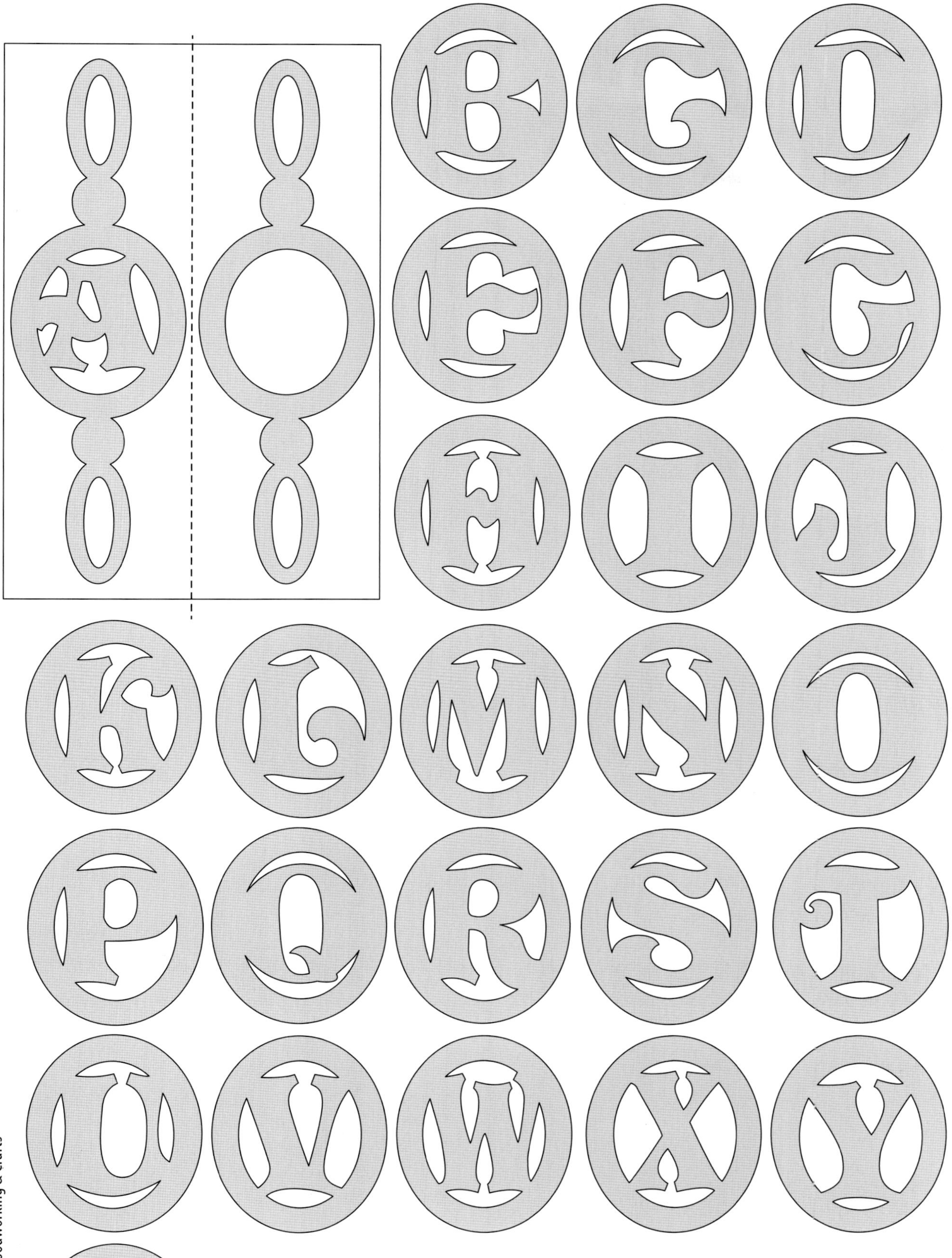

Monogram ornament patterns

Enlarge to 133% or desired size.

*To see more of Sue Mey's work
visit www.scrollsawartist.com.*

Intarsia
ORNAMENTS

By Judy Gale Roberts

Materials & Tools

Materials:
See pattern legends on page 13 for suggested wood species
Bell:
- Light wood, ¾" (19mm) thick: 3" x 6" (7.6cm x 15.2cm)
- Medium-light wood, ¾" (19mm) thick: 2½" (6.4cm) square
- Medium wood, ¾" (19mm) thick: 2" x 4" (5.1cm x 10.2cm)
- Medium-dark wood, ¾" (19mm) thick: 2" x 3" (5.1cm x 7.6cm)
- Hardboard tempered on both sides, ⅛" (3mm) thick: backing board, 4¾" x 5 (12.1cm x 12.7cm)

Bear:
- White wood, ¾" (19mm) thick: 2½" 6.4cm) square
- Medium wood, ¾" (19mm) thick: ½" x 1½" (1.3cm x 3.8cm)
- Medium-dark wood, ¾" (19mm) thick: 4" x 6" (10.2cm x 15.2cm)
- Dark wood, ¾" (19mm) thick: 1½" (3.8cm) square
- Dowel, ³⁄₁₆" (5mm) dia.: scraps walnut (eyes)
- Toothpick (pupils)
- Hardboard tempered on both sides, ⅛" (3mm) thick: backing board 4" x 5¾" (10.2cm x 14.6cm)

Cat:
- Light wood, ¾" (19mm) thick: 4" x 6" (10.2cm x 15.2cm)
- Medium-light wood, ¾" (19mm) thick: 4" (10.2cm) square
- Medium wood, ¾" (19mm) thick: 4" (10.2cm) square
- Medium-dark wood, ¾" (19mm) thick: 2" (5.1cm) square
- Dowel, ³⁄₁₆" (5mm) dia.: scraps walnut (eyes)
- Toothpick (pupils)
- Hardboard tempered on both sides, ⅛" (3mm) thick: backing board, 3½" x 8½" (8.9cm x 21.6cm)

General:
- Glue stick or temporary-bond spray adhesive
- Finish, such as polyurethane gel
- Glue: tacky; wood
- Tape: double-sided light-traffic carpet; masking

Tools:
- Scroll saw blades: #3 or #5 skip reverse-tooth
- Sanders: small inflatable; flexible drum with 80-, 120-, 180-, & 220-grit sleeves
- Drill with ¹⁄₁₆" (2mm) bit
- Foam brush
- Woodburner with tips/pens

The author used these products for the project. Substitute your choice of brands, tools, and materials as desired.

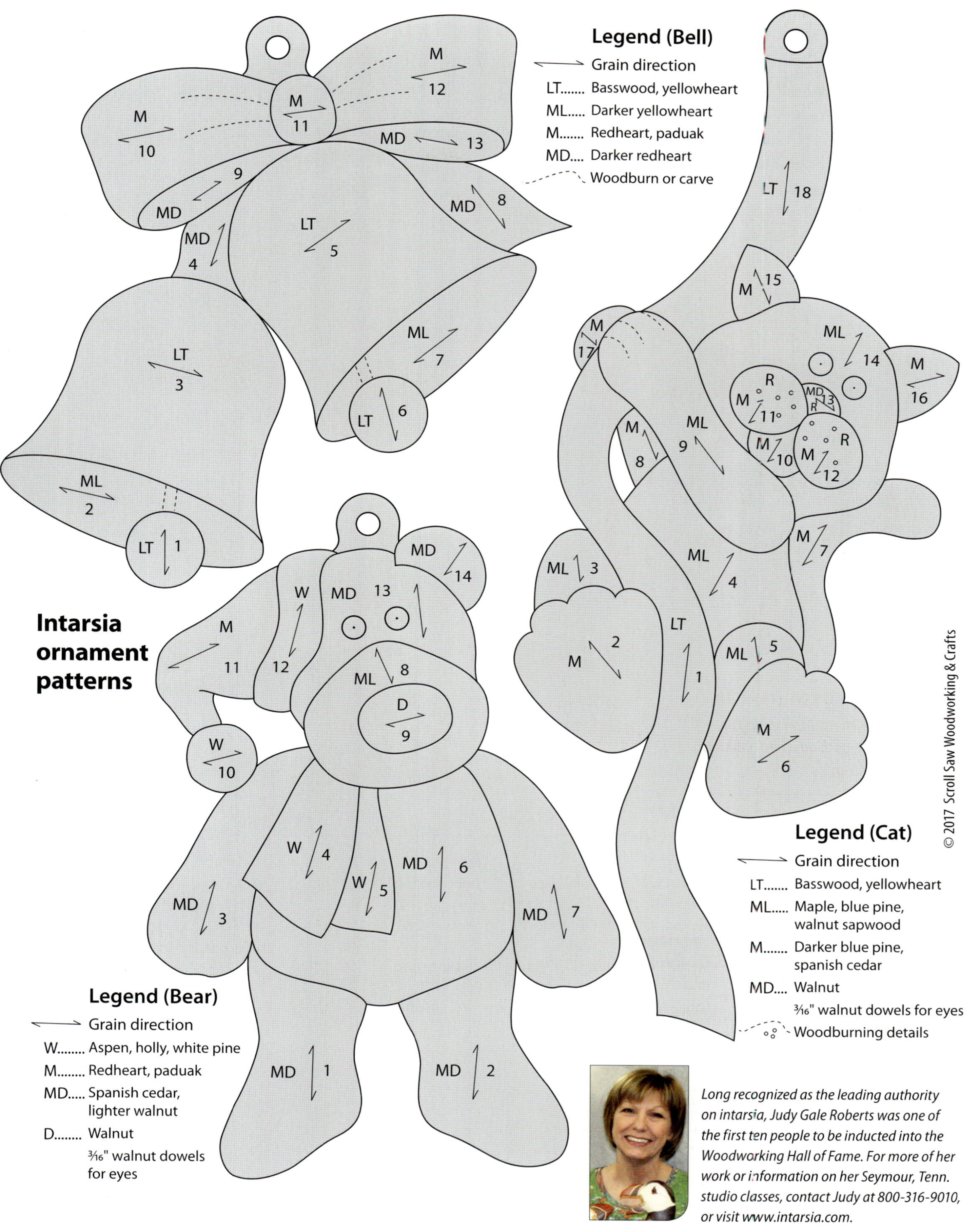

Intarsia ornament patterns

Legend (Bell)
Grain direction
LT....... Basswood, yellowheart
ML..... Darker yellowheart
M....... Redheart, paduak
MD.... Darker redheart
Woodburn or carve

Legend (Cat)
Grain direction
LT....... Basswood, yellowheart
ML..... Maple, blue pine, walnut sapwood
M....... Darker blue pine, spanish cedar
MD.... Walnut
3/16" walnut dowels for eyes
Woodburning details

Legend (Bear)
Grain direction
W........ Aspen, holly, white pine
M........ Redheart, paduak
MD..... Spanish cedar, lighter walnut
D........ Walnut
3/16" walnut dowels for eyes

Long recognized as the leading authority on intarsia, Judy Gale Roberts was one of the first ten people to be inducted into the Woodworking Hall of Fame. For more of her work or information on her Seymour, Tenn. studio classes, contact Judy at 800-316-9010, or visit www.intarsia.com.

Christmas Tea Light Holders

By Sue Mey
Cut by Rolf Beuttenmuller

Tea light holder patterns

Front/back - Cut 1 each

Enlarge to 133%
or desired size.

*To see more of Sue Mey's work
visit www.scrollsawartist.com.*

Snow Family Puzzles

By Judy and Dave Peterson
Cut by Leldon Maxcy
Painted by Kristen Scanlan

If you prefer to leave your puzzle unpainted, cut it from maple and use a woodburner to add the detail lines.

Materials & Tools

Materials:
- Pine: ¾" to 1" (1.9cm to 2.5cm) thick: man, 3¼" x 6¼" (8.3cm x 15.9cm); woman, 3¾" x 6" (9.5cm x 15.2cm); boy, 3" x 5" (7.6cm x 12.7cm); girl, 3¼" x 6" (8.3cm x 15.2cm)
- Sandpaper
- Sealer, such as Krylon spray finish
- Acrylic paint

Tools:
- Scroll saw blades: #5 reverse-tooth
- Flexible sander, such as a Sand-o-Flex

The author used these products for the project. Substitute your choice of brands, tools, and materials as desired.

A former teacher and librarian, Judy Peterson found her niche in life as a woodworker. She sells her puzzles at art shows around the country. Her husband, Dave, runs the record-keeping side of the business. Together they have written several books, which are available at www. foxchapelpublishing.com.

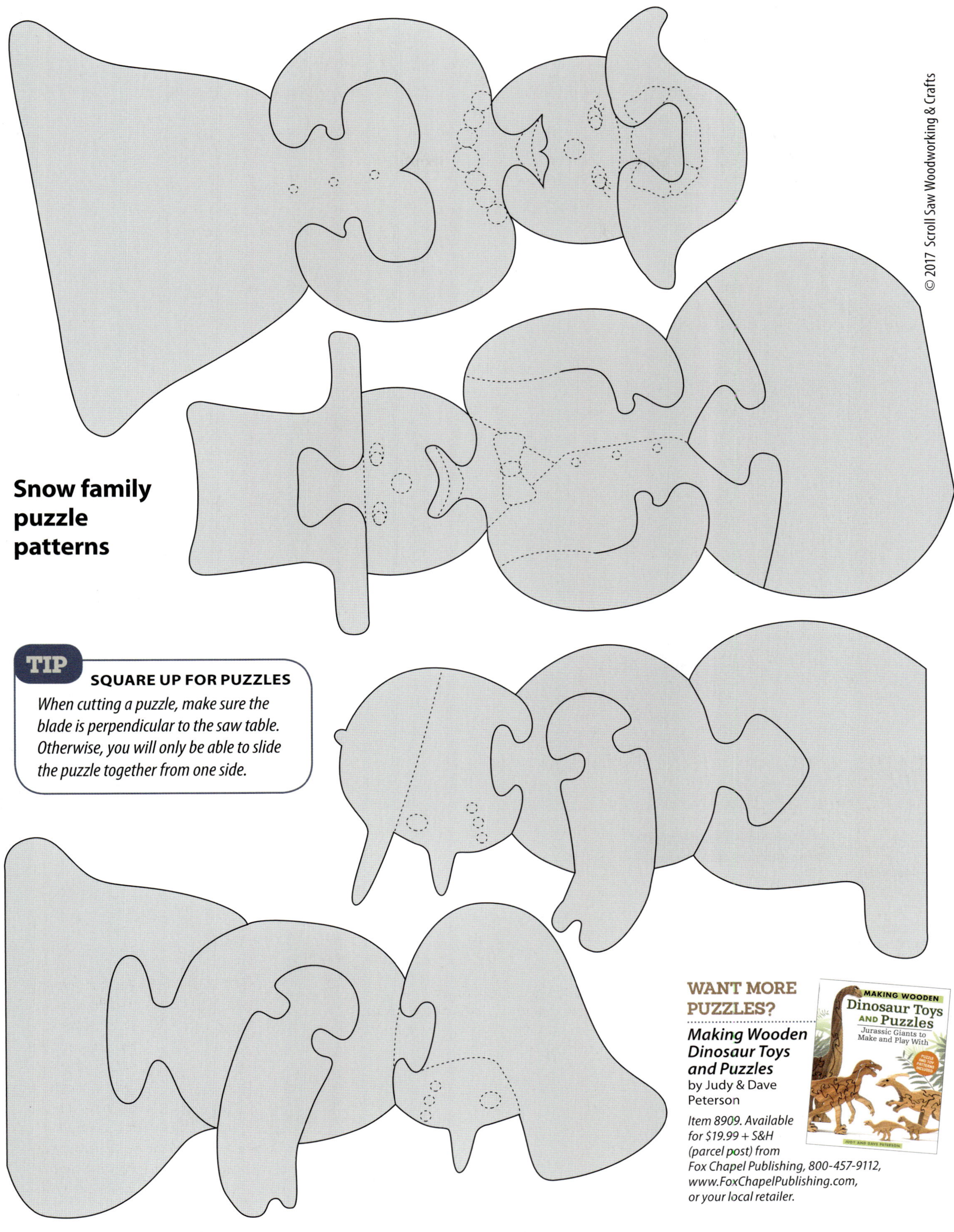

Snow family puzzle patterns

TIP

SQUARE UP FOR PUZZLES

When cutting a puzzle, make sure the blade is perpendicular to the saw table. Otherwise, you will only be able to slide the puzzle together from one side.

FRETWORK
Advent Candle Holder

By Sue Mey
Cut by Leldon Maxcy

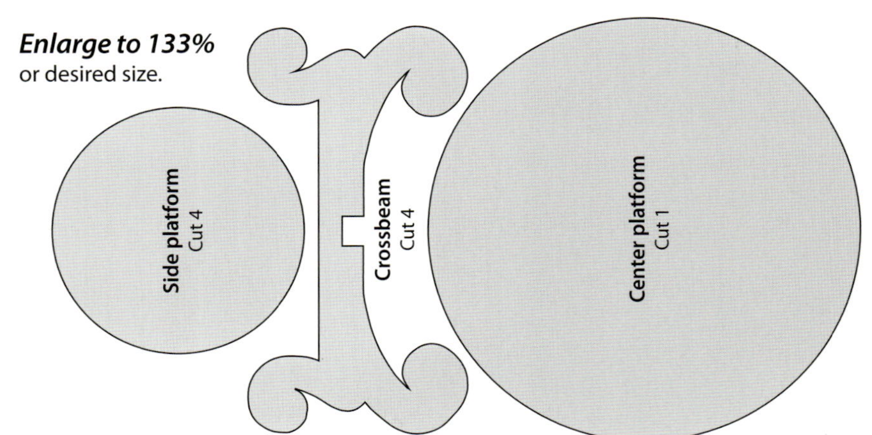

Materials:
- Wood, ¼" (6mm) thick: frames, 2 each 5¼" x 13½" (13.3cm x 34.3cm); crossbeams, 4 each 1¾" x 3⅛" (4.4cm x 7.9cm); center platform, 3¼" (8.3cm) square; side platforms, 4 each, 2" (5.1cm) square
- Sandpaper
- Glue: wood or cyanoacrylate (CA)

Tools:
- Scroll saw blades: #3 reverse-tooth
- Drill with bits: assorted small
- Needle files or fingernail files
- Clamps

The author used these products for the project. Substitute your choice of brands, tools, and materials as desired.

Enlarge to 133% or desired size.

Side platform Cut 4

Crossbeam Cut 4

Center platform Cut 1

To see more of Sue Mey's work visit www.scrollsawartist.com.

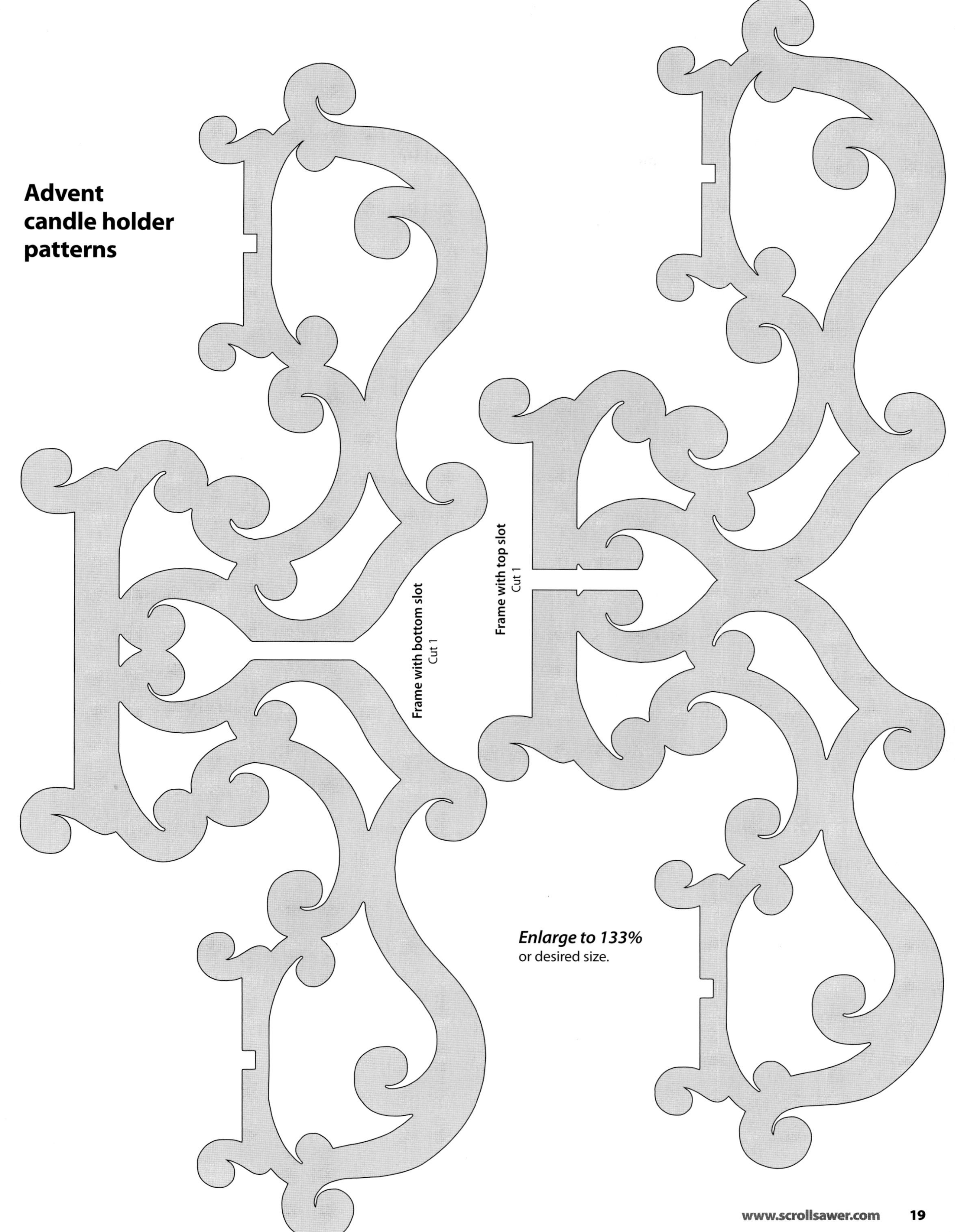

Advent
candle holder
patterns

Frame with bottom slot
Cut 1

Frame with top slot
Cut 1

Enlarge to 133%
or desired size.

Penguin Segmentation

By Frank Droege

Materials & Tools

Materials:
- Pine, ¾" (1.9cm) thick: 8⅜" x 10¾" (21.3cm x 27.3cm)
- Acrylic paint: Navy blue, medium blue, light blue, white, yellow, black, gray
- Sandpaper
- Wood glue
- Baltic birch plywood, ⅛" (3mm) thick: backing board, 8⅜" x 10¾" (21.3cm x 27.3cm)

Tools:
- Scroll saw blades: #3 reverse-tooth
- Paintbrushes
- Clamps

The author used these products for the project. Substitute your choice of brands, tools, and materials as desired.

In addition to designing scroll saw patterns, the late Frank Droege won numerous awards as a traditional painter.

Penguin segmentation pattern

Enlarge to 111%
or desired size.

JOY
Word Art

By John A. Nelson
Cut by Leldon Maxcy

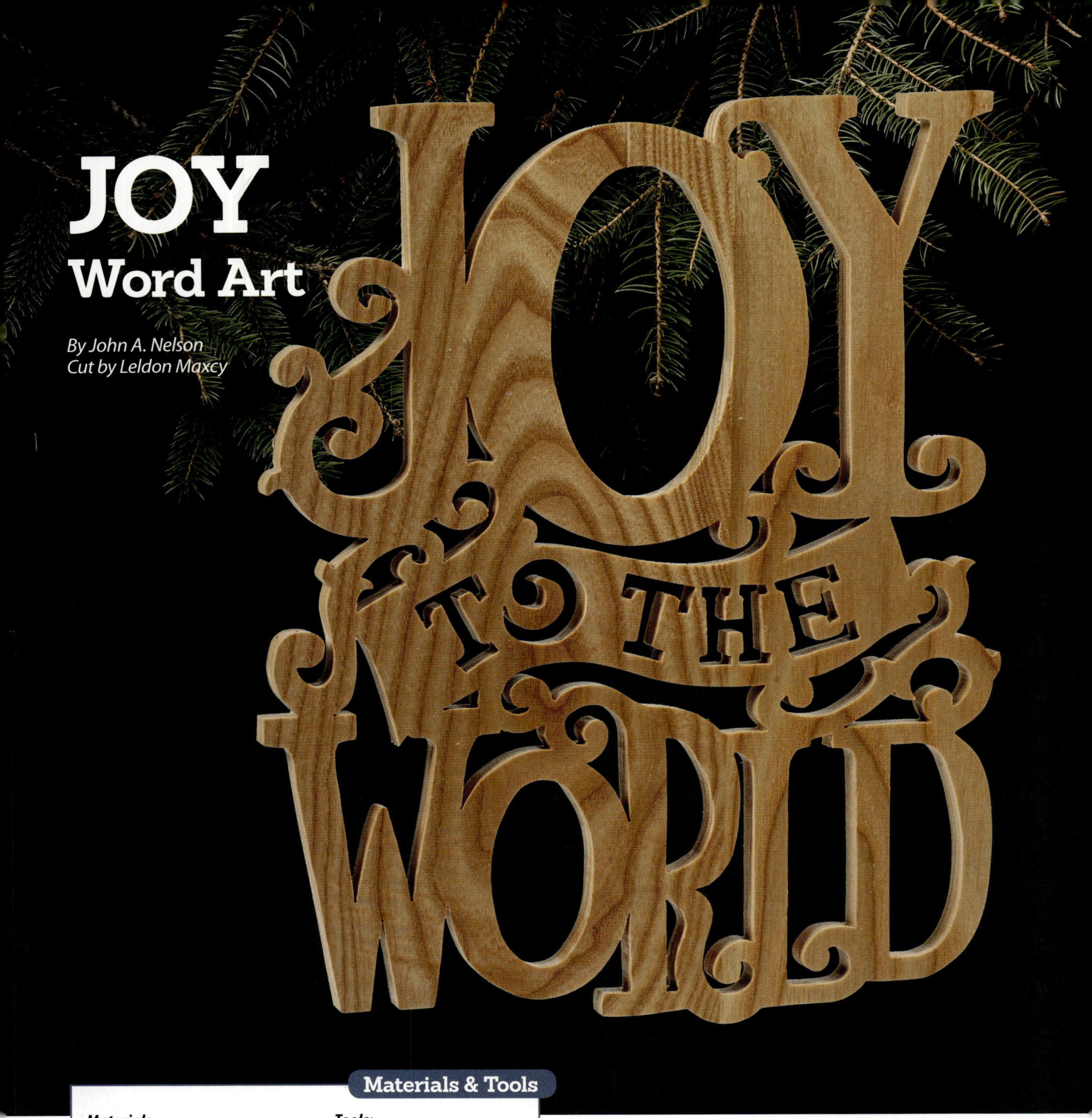

Materials & Tools

Materials:
- Wood, ¼" (6mm) thick: 8" x 10" (20.3cm x 25.4cm)
- Baltic birch plywood, ⅛" (3mm) thick: backing board (optional), 8" x 10" (20.3cm x 25.4cm)
- Sandpaper
- Wood glue

Tools:
- Scroll saw blades: #1 reverse-tooth
- Drill with bits: assorted small
- Clamps

The author used these products for the project. Substitute your choice of brands, tools, and materials as desired.

John A. Nelson is the author of Fox Chapel's popular Scroll Saw Workbook, *available at www.foxchapelpublishing.com.*

JOY
TO THE WORLD

Mistletoe
DECORATION

By Jacob and Wayne Fowler

Jacob Fowler designed his first scroll saw project when he was five years old. He now spends most of his time designing fantasy and animal patterns. Wayne Fowler has published nearly 150 articles since 1998. His work has won awards at a local craft guild and several science fiction conventions.

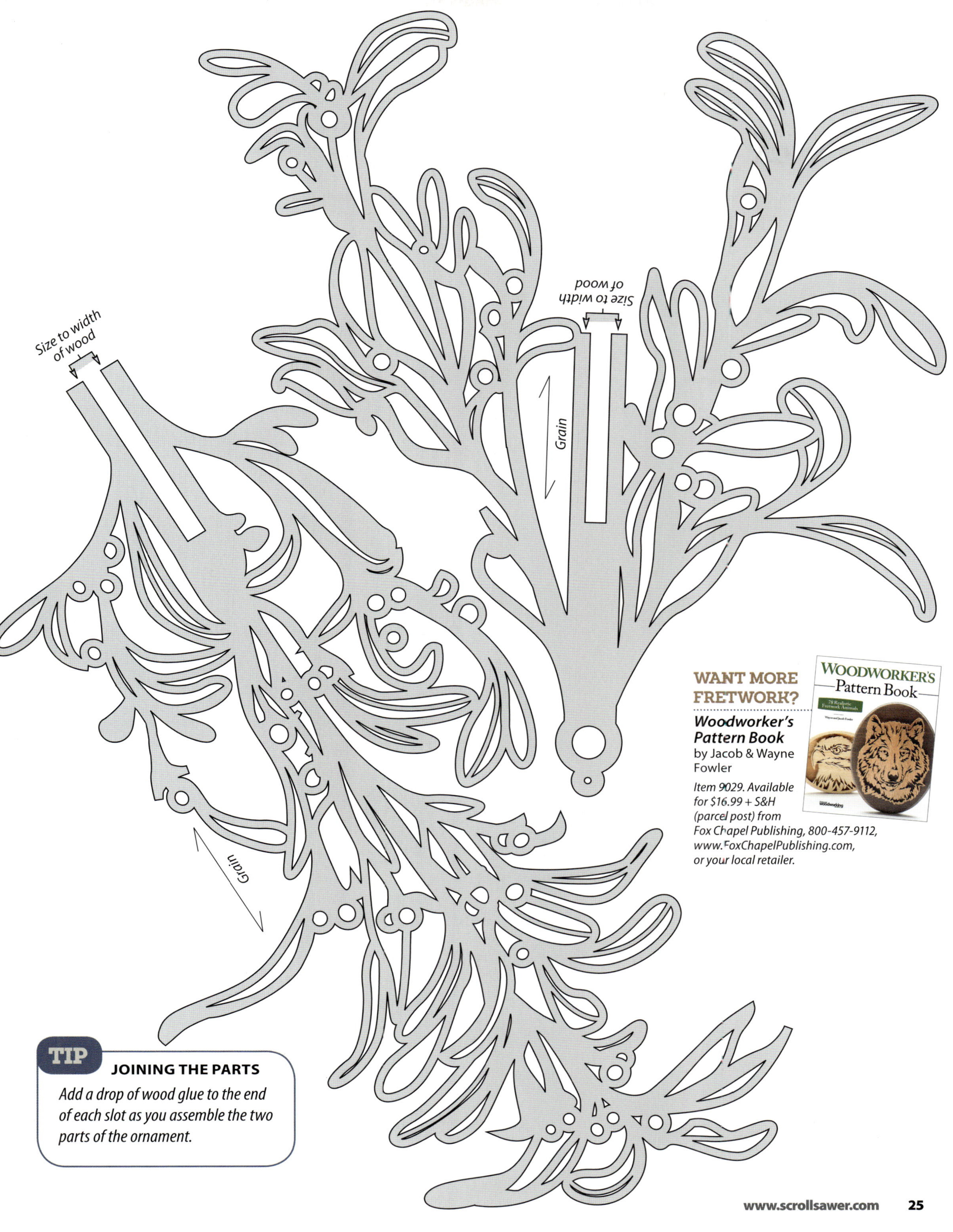

TIP

JOINING THE PARTS

Add a drop of wood glue to the end of each slot as you assemble the two parts of the ornament.

Snowman Candleholder

By Paul Meisel

TIP

MAKE THINNER WOOD

Instead of getting a piece of ¼" (6mm)-thick wood just for the nose, cut the nose from scrap ¾" (1.9cm)-thick stock and rip it down to ¼" (6mm) thick.

Assembly drawing

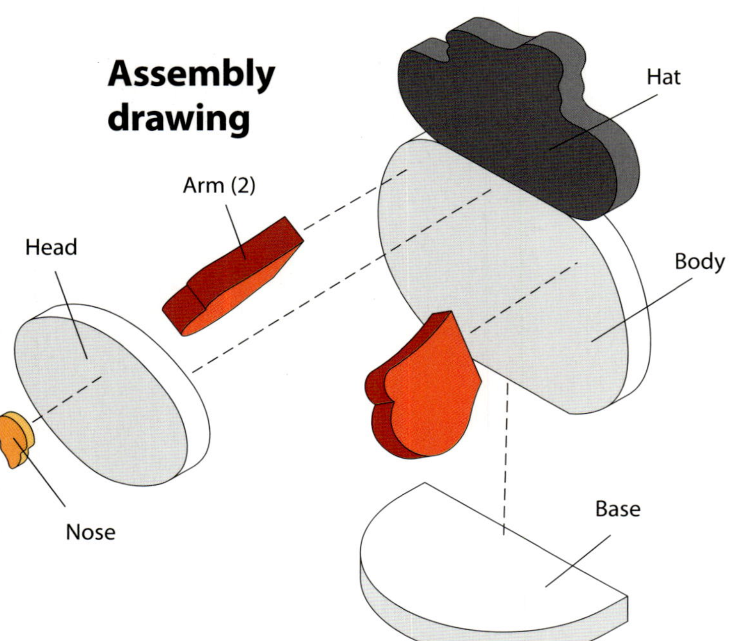

Materials & Tools

Materials:
- Pine, ¾" (1.9cm) thick: 7" x 24" (17.8cm x 61cm)
- Sandpaper
- Glue
- Wood screws: 6 each #6 x 1⅝" (4.1cm) (6278)*
- Acrylic paint, such as Delta Ceramcoat*: black (02506), white (02505), orange (02042), red (02507), green (02421), yellow (02504), blue (07005)
- Wood sealer, such as Delta Ceramcoat (#07005)*
- Paint marker: black fine line (3261)*

The author used these products for the project. Substitute your choice of brands, tools, and materials as desired.

Tools:
- Scroll saw blades: #5 reverse-tooth
- Clamps
- Screwdriver
- Paintbrushes

SPECIAL SOURCES:
The items above marked with an asterisk (*) are available from Meisel Hardware Specialties. Call 1-800-441-9870 or visit their website, www.meiselwoodhobby.com.

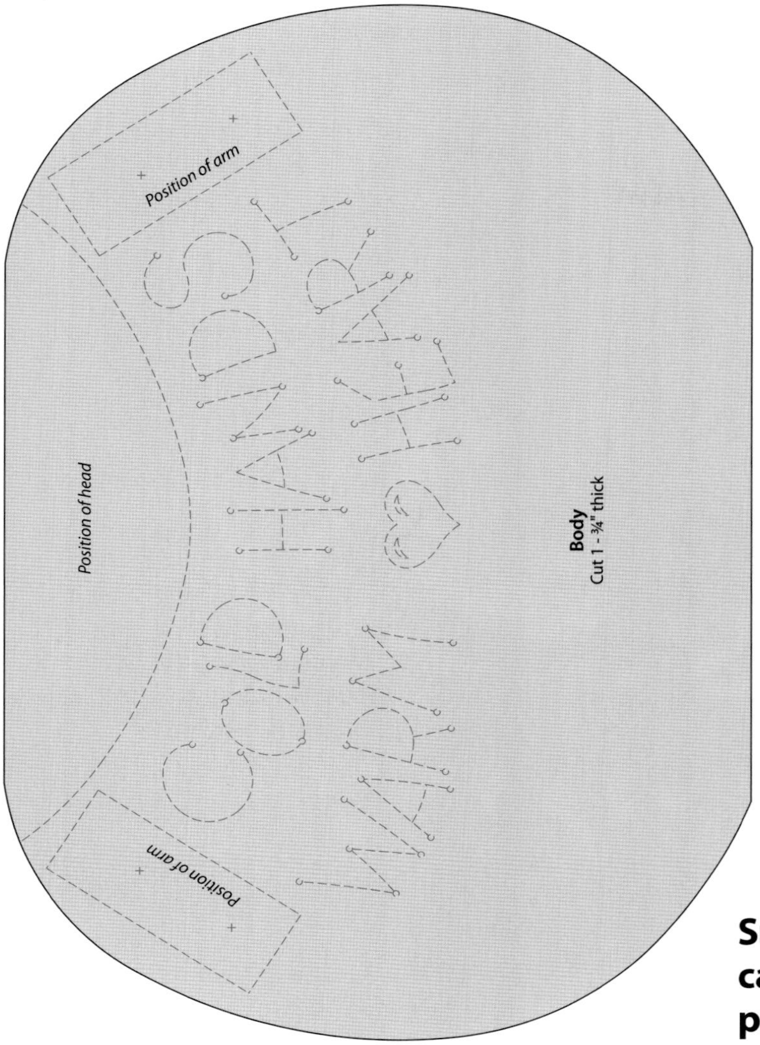

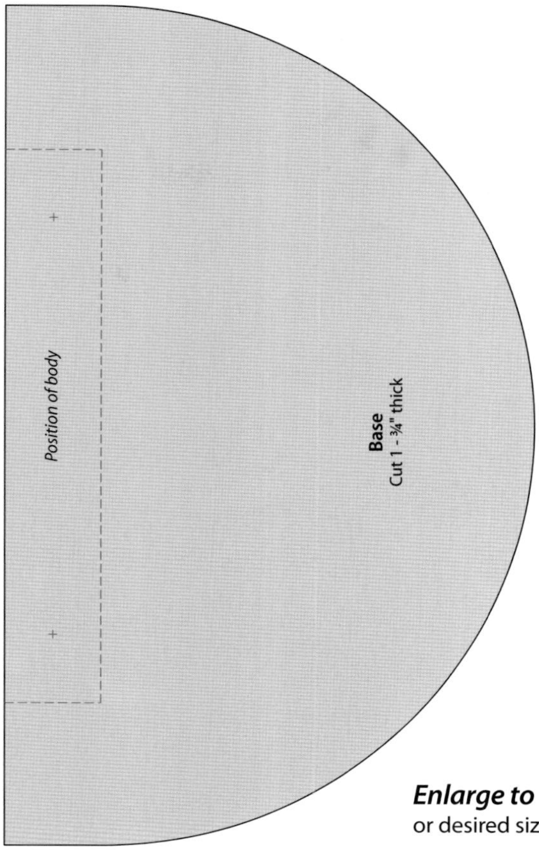

Enlarge to 150%
or desired size.

Snowman candleholder patterns

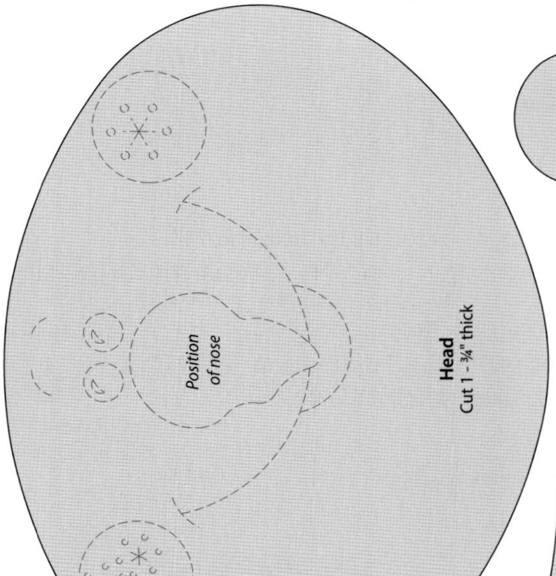

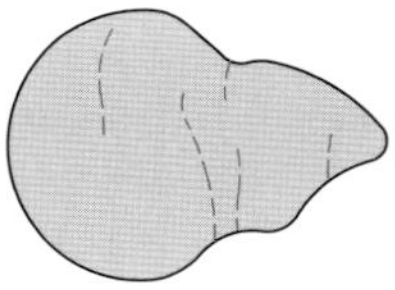

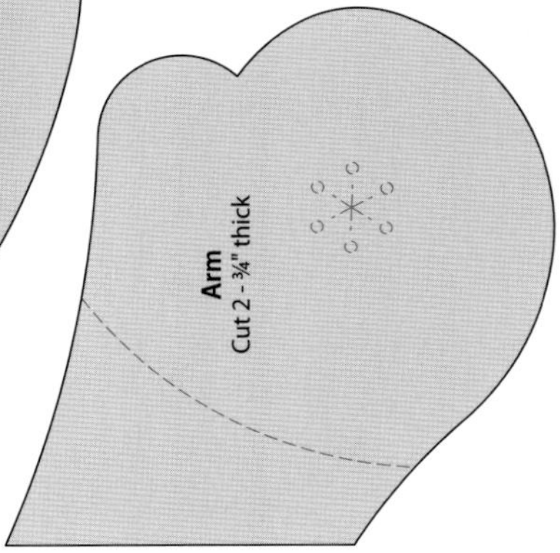

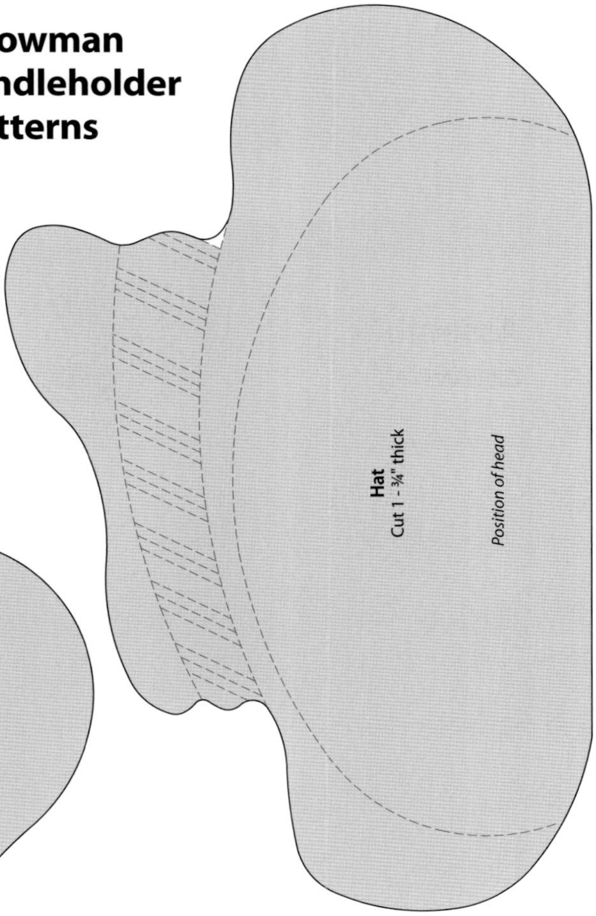

Fretwork Sleigh Centerpiece

By John A. Nelson
Cut by Rolf Beuttenmuller

Parts List

	Part	Quantity	Materials	Dimensions
A	Side	2	Wood, ¼" (6mm) thick	5½" x 9½" (14cm x 24.1cm)
B	Back	1	Wood, ¼" (6mm) thick	5" x 6" (12.7cm x 15.2cm)
C	Front	1	Wood, ¼" (6mm) thick	3½" x 4¾" (8.9cm x 12.1cm)
D	Top	1	Wood, ¼" (6mm) thick	2" x 5¼" (5.1cm x 13.3cm)
E	Front support	2	Wood, ¼" (6mm) thick	1½" (3.8cm) square
F	Front rail	1	Dowel, ⅛" (3mm) dia.	3¼" (8.3cm) long
G	Side embellishment	2	Wood, ¼" (6mm) thick	2" x 3" (5.1cm x 7.6cm)
H	Support pin	4	Dowel, ⅛" (3mm) dia.	½" (1.3cm) long
I	Runner	2	Wood, ¼" (6mm) thick	4¾" x 12½" (12.1cm x 31.8cm)
J	Runner support	2	Wood, ¼" (6mm) thick	2" x 4¼" (5.1cm x 10.8cm)
K	Tow bar	1	Dowel, ¼" (6mm) dia.	3¼" (8.3cm) long
L	Bottom	1	Wood, ¼" (6mm) thick	5½" x 10½" (14cm x 26.7cm)
M	Back support	2	Wood, ¼" (6mm) thick	1¾" x 2" (4.4cm x 5.1cm)
N	Back rail	1	Dowel, ⅛" (3mm) dia.	3¼" (8.3cm) long

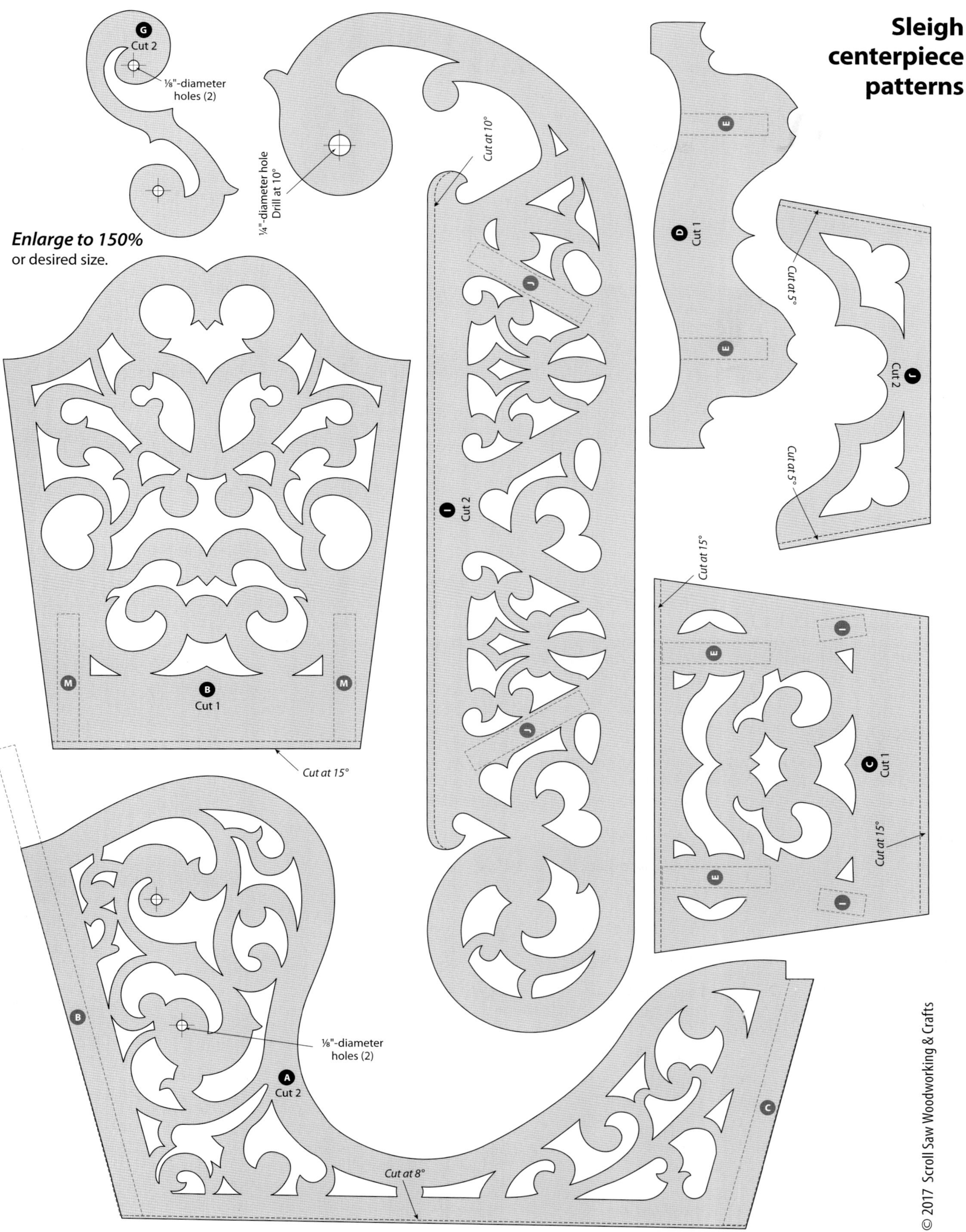
G
Cut 2
⅛"-diameter
holes (2)
¼"-diameter hole
Drill at 10°
Enlarge to 150%
or desired size.
Cut at 10°
D Cut 1
E
E
Cut at 5°
L Cut 2
Cut at 5°
J
I Cut 2
J
Cut at 15°
E
F Cut 1
Cut at 15°
I
E
I
B Cut 1
M
M
Cut at 15°
B
⅛"-diameter
holes (2)
A Cut 2
C
Cut at 8°

A

M

B

L
Cut 1

C

Front ⟶

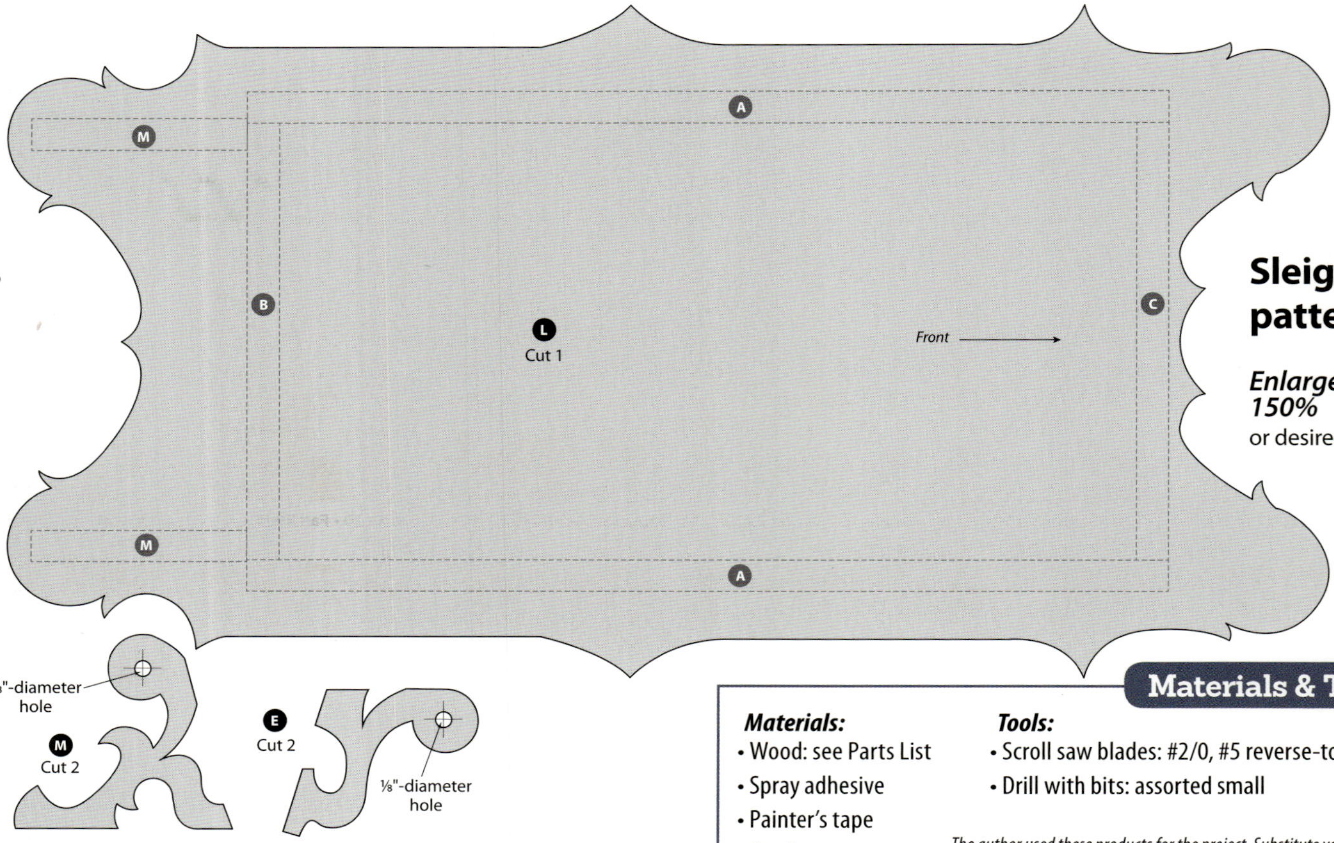

Sleigh patterns

Enlarge to 150% or desired size.

⅛"-diameter hole

M
Cut 2

E
Cut 2

⅛"-diameter hole

Reindeer Ornament

By Jacob and Wayne Fowler

Reindeer ornament pattern

Materials & Tools

Materials:
- Wood: ¼" (6mm) thick: 4½" x 5" (11.4cm x 12.7cm)
- Sandpaper: 220 or 320 grit
- Spray adhesive: temporary-bond
- Tape: clear packaging
- Finish: oil

Tools:
- Scroll saw blades: #3 reverse-tooth
- Drill press with bits: assorted small
- Sander (optional): belt or disc sander

The author used these products for the project. Substitute your choice of brands, tools, and materials as desired.